Leaf to Leaf

Su Nayanæ

BookLeaf Publishing

India | USA | UK

Presentation by *BookLeaf Publishing*

Web: www.bookleafpub.com

E-mail: info@bookleafpub.com

ISBN: 9789363316430

First edition 2024

*To Nirmal—the artist, poet, my mom, mentor,
and muse.*

ACKNOWLEDGEMENT

The entire credit for this serendipitous till goes to my dear mother, who planted the seed that sprouted only after her demise. I believe it is her voice that speaks through me.

The final push came from my sons, Tushar and Shaurya, who have always supported my decisions, and from my nephews, Karmenyae and Shreyes, who continue to be my biggest cheerleaders.

Editing credit: Shaurya Malik

PREFACE

Mere musings on my journey toward self-realisation, at the tender age of almost 60, somehow found poetic appreciation from a few fellow fledglings. Some loved me, a few accepted me, many challenged me, and some even deserted me—each encounter forcing the hand of my individual evolution. For all of this, I'm forever indebted.

I'm grateful for the shaky start. Brittle as it may have been, history bears witness to how my foundation stone has grown more robust over time, weathered yet strengthened, perhaps even because of the weathering itself.

This seemingly docile yet irresistibly charged stream of consciousness is now yours. So, enjoy the surface. Explore the depths. Dive into the turbulence, flow along the rapids, swirl into the tiny whirlpools. And when you resurface, take a breather on an island adorned with flowering cacti and giant dry leaves. You might emerge quenched, or perhaps thirstier. But define it not, dam it not— just flow along and feel its soul, the *rooh*.

INDEX

Infinite.. 1

A poem dawns.. 3

Poetree.. 5

The flowering cactus - The Old Monk.............. 7

Yogin...9

The last leaf.. 12

The beach of memories.................................. 14

I'm a figure of 8..16

Past, present, future and yoga.........................18

The drop..20

Life's lemons.. 22

Purpose...25

Words and a tear... 27

Iffy..29

Past the prime.. 31

The Giant... 32

The Noise...34

Sorrow and love..36

Moksha and dreams......................................38

Irritation..40

The Buddha moment...................................... 42

Even Better..45

From outdoors to in...................................... 46

On my deathbed...48

Me..51

Leaf to Leaf.. 53

The night..55

SHAKTI.. 57

Longevity..59

Relativity.. 61

The Fable.. 63

Together, alone.................................... 65

He blows hot he blows cold....................67

Two Swans..69

Equation of love................................... 71

Nirvana here and now...........................73

End..75

Life is a bicycle.................................... 77

Suicide... 79

Rasa... 80

A night swallowed................................83

The gift.. 85

Infinite

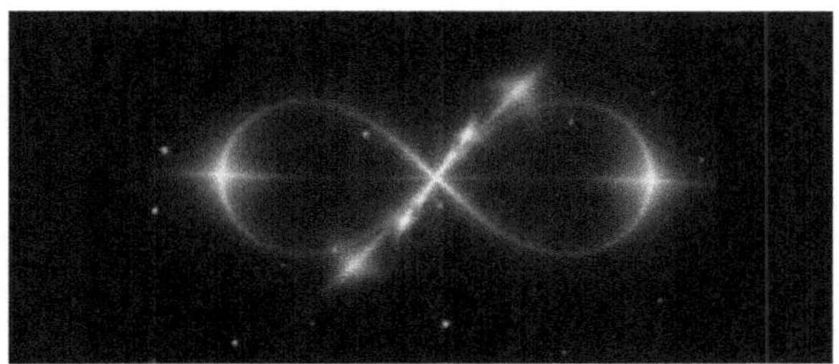

Some thuds and kicks
Brought the world
Down
For the hourglass!

The figure of 8
It remained
What it was.

The attempt
To tilt the balance
Or stop altogether.
The Ebb and flow
Of the sparkles
Within
Grew fiercer.

The hourglass of 8,
Was no longer straight.

Fallen?
Ahhh..it lay there,
Decrepit.

Gathering its ashes,
It became,
Infinite.

-Su

A poem dawns

A poem,
Is not a work of art.

It's the nectar
Of the soul,
Dripping
But occasionally,
To savour, to behold.

You don't create it,
It dawns upon!
Like a fairy godmother,
Straight from the heavens beyond.

Of course, add some stars

By the art of editing,
Transform 'good' into
'Great' writing.

Revisit a poem,
That once dawned.
Add some tinsel
to the yarn spawned.
Pick and choose words
That don't add much;
Replace, refine,
and pack more punch.

Read the poem out aloud.
Offish? does anything sound
Adjust till smoothly it flows—
You could be the next Bard,
Who knows!

Great poets aren't just born;
Chiseling, is the art,
On what once dawned.

-Su

Poetree

The innocent inflorescence
thought
The bee was her bae.

Bee was not to be,
He went flitting,
Flirting,
with the next prey.

He sings
Songs of love—
The meaning?

Know not he does

"Mi amor!"
He calls his next.
Not "lover"! No!
He's amorous at best.

Nectar he seeks,
Needs he knows.
Whosoever grants the basics,
His attention, he bestows.

The higher love
That the flower knew,
Beyond desires low,
Is for but a very few.

-says Su

The flowering cactus - The Old Monk

I haven't paid attention
In a while
To this dry, prickly monk.

Haven't I been busy
Tending and pruning
The fledglings,
Raising their tender,
Colourful limbs
All around?

Isn't Spring the season
Of new birth,
New growth,
New dance?

Come winter,
I'll have
A soulful
Tête-à-tête
With my old, loyal monk.

But no!
The monk decides
He can't be ignored for so long.
So what if he has no
Bright tendrils
To spread in my direction?
He's decided
To catch my attention—
Sprouting a sky
And winking
With its help,
A fluorescent hi!
Through the corner of my eye.

-Su

Yogin

Those who feel
That yoga and spirituality are oh-so-boring,
Are oh-so-wrong.

A Yogi is *Anandmayi*—
Full of love,
Fearless, hateless,
A treasure trove.

For happiness—
Some indulge in
Sex, parties, substances, drinks,
Intrigue, perversion, politics.

Money, power, lust, deceit, lies,
To get the high
Soaked in the sins.
Without them,
You find them in gutters,
 in the trashbins.

Yog is not
Dressing codes severe,
Nagasadhus!
On them, a thong wouldn't adhere.

And then!
There! The perv!
In the garb of gentlemen and women,
What rubbish they serve.

Satvikta-
is a state of the mind,
Not of name and fame,
Only of the soul so kind.

Our temples of yore
Had ascetics, royals, and commoners galore—
Alongside erotic figurines, poses
That you may abhor.

Everything is normal, healthy,
A part of life.

Nothing is titillating,
If pure is the mind.

In times so ancient, so great,
Folks would keep
Most of the body bare—
That booted, suited, stiff pained
Caricatures of today
Wouldn't dare

Women were not covered
In veils to earlobes,
Or hiding every inch
Behind burly robes.

For they were not
Mere objects petty—
They had an equal, respectable
Status in society.

Experience the high!
Have pure joy.
Be a *yogi*—
Not a parasitic, mindless decoy.

-Su

soulosunayanae

The last leaf

In the dark, dark night,
The fog made the neighbours invisible.
My house-gate stood lonely,
Uninterested in my arrival.
Dogs barked at my unidentified existence.
But…

Hey!

This giant,
Beautiful,
Subtle
Leaf.
Wafting softly under my feet,
Smiling back,
Whispering
In its gentle rustle:
"Love is here!"
Albeit,
In this figment,
In this moment!

-Su

The beach of memories

I was sitting on dry sands,
away from the humdrum
of naughty ripples—
superficial,
pretentious,
colourful on borrowed colour
of the mighty heavens.

I watched from afar,

Having left the storms behind—
The whirlpools of
Power,
Churning and collapsing,
Rising and falling.
Let the rivulets
Play their never-ending
Power game,
Pretending to win,
Rising in fragile glory,
Only to fall flat
On the face of the ocean.

Why, oh why, O lovely surf,
Did you come
To engulf me
In forgotten turmoils,
And spoil
My reverie?

-Su

I'm a figure of 8

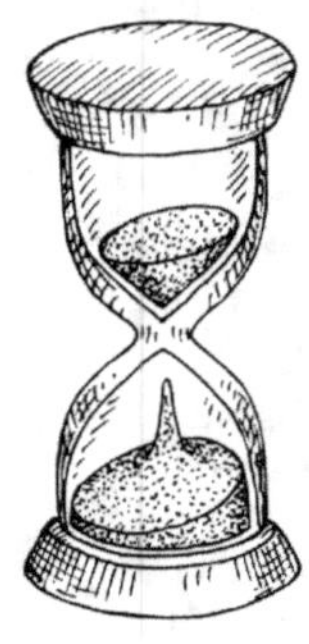

I am a figure of 8,
Learnt it quite late.

Happiness appeared to be a full circle,
Turned out to be a big zero.

Up, up, up goes the bubble,
Only to burst—
The sparkles come twinkling down.

The 8 catches every grain of sparkle
In its downward circle,
Never to let the tiniest
Pearl go out
Get wasted.
It starts its countdown

In the hourglass
Of time.
And lo!
All the pearls trickle down,
To rise up again,
Untouched like
A lotus
In
The ebb and flow
Of the murky
Continuum.

-Su

Past, present, future and yoga

The memory is your past,
But it's not completely lost.
The future, not just a figment of imagination,
It holds the hope, the excitement of creation.

The harmonious interweaving

Of the memories into your imagination,
To flow into a luminous NOW,
This is Yoga, the culmination.

Energy is always conserved:
Create, destroy, or lay
unperturbed.
To synthesize something living,
Vibrant, immense,
Out of frail elements
Is the miracle of being.

Does it now make sense
The enigma of past, present, and future tense,
Rendered perfect
To uphold nature's
Balance.

-Su

The drop

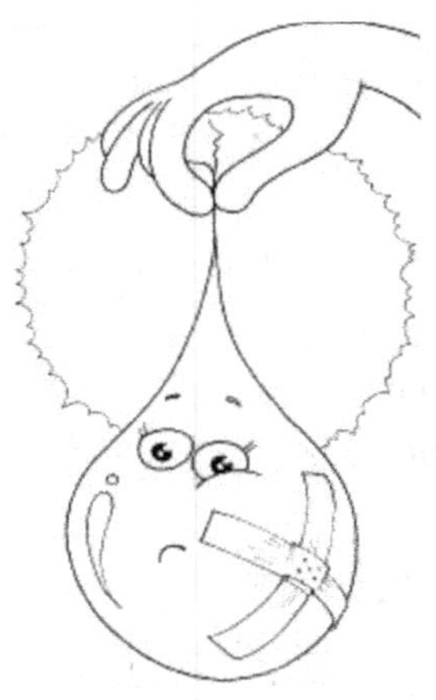

A drop is inextinguishable, like Atma,
Never destroyed, burnt or dirtied
It waits for you to reclaim it.

If the lotus fails
To turn it into a pearl,
Itself thus,
become the swarn kamal,
Iridescent with its glow.
But drops the drop
Into the mud,
To wallow.

Lo, the soiled drop

Rises from the muck,
Which thought it absorbed
And ended its luck.

Sadly departing from its lotus,
Leaving the greens below.
Ascending the heavens,
With the clouds,
To flow.

Come rain,
It shall return again.

-Su

Life's lemons

I'd thought,
"तोड़ूं या निहारूं"
To pluck or to adore,
Even when they were
lemons,
Served by a life, oh so sore.

Love was brimming over—
Upon poor life
and her limitations,
And upon
Those shiny
Green globules,
Gleaming with perfection.

Your heart,

Mind it!
Is not governed
By the vagaries
Of the world's manipulation.

The globelets grew
And grew—
They just wouldn't stop.
Such
Was the love
In my heart,

Complimenting,
Touching,
Fondling,
The green sour lemons
In my palms,
Never
Daring to pluck them apart
From the fleshy
Lap of the mothering plant,
Despite her thorns.

Lo! Behold!
Magic began to unfold!
The sour bitterness
Transformed
Into sweetness manifold
For

The lemons
Transformed into
Limes,
The likes of which
You might never hold.

Life, my darlings,
Is what you ask
And make of it—
Nothing less,
Nothing more.
It's your task!

-Su

Purpose

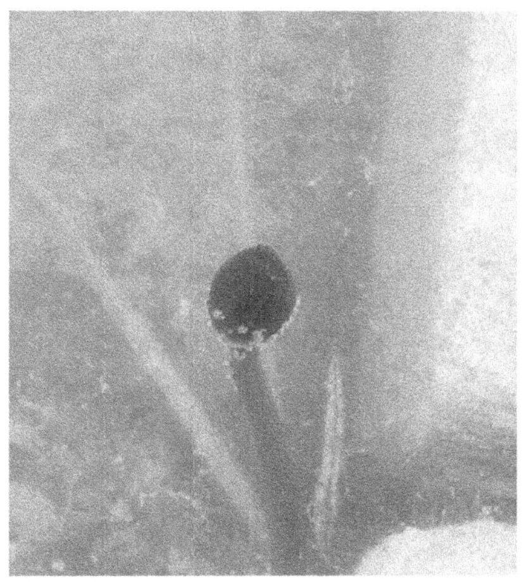

The bejewelled bud
Beneath the veil,

Ready to burst—
Out of the hazy depths—
To
Kiss the Sun
With its expanded limbs and lips

Will you call it
In full bloom,
Or broken?

Will you pluck it,
Or leave it untouched
To spread
Its beauty, its fragrance?

Will you place it
On the god's pedestal,
Or crush it
To its last petal?

Whatever!
Does it care?

Its purpose
Is to bloom—
TODAY.

-Su

Words and a tear

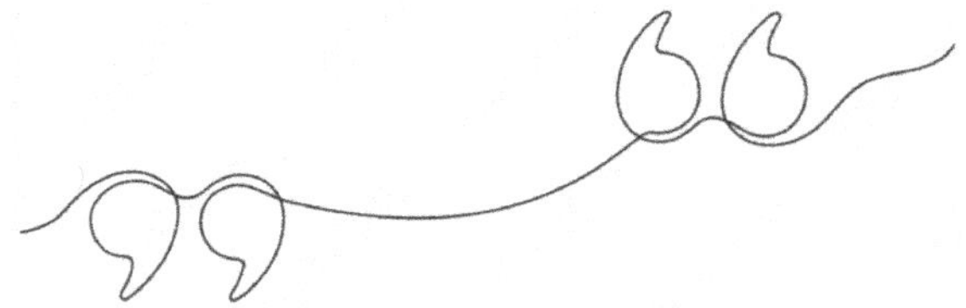

I am a talker,
Yet they've labelled me
The quiet one.

I talk to myself—
Of life, plants, honeybees,
Stars, and the Sun.

I like to talk,
Only with sensible company,
Hard to find some.

Common sense,
So uncommon, you see.
Alone, thus, is fun.

Darling, darling,
Without words, I'll hear you clear—
Let the time come.

No words, no rhyme,
Just oodles of love and a tear,
When we become one!

-Su

Iffy

The world,
Is a jail.
Yes,
Pretty icky and sticky.

Fiery, hellish dungeons—
Oh, they scare
You truly.
Unscrupulous crooks and fiends
Roar and roam about freely.

But, they all
Would perish
In a jiffy.

If…
The kind souls,
The ones who provide succour,
Too
Become,
Iffy!

-Su

Past the prime

I am the Sun,
past my prime.
The Sun at its
prime, at noon,
is for everybody.
It catches everything.
The harsh glare
That won't spare,
Even when you hide
from it.

But to catch the aura
Of the rich,
mellow, colourful,
soothing, beautiful,
vibrant, playful
Sun at dusk,
you have to make an effort
to reach out to it.
-Su

The Giant

That giant,
  Gently swaying,
    Peeping from my
      Window on the third floor.

Reaching for the sky,
  Yet softly grounded,
    Welcomes me,
      While hosting another score.

The chirping
        Of birds,
  Quiet rustle

Of butterflies,
    And insects unheard.

Its leaves glistening
    In the rain that pattered away,
  Undulating wind
      Makes this mammoth sway.
Teaches IT—
    To not waste its welcome,
        But sit in silence and pray.

Pray, while the limbs
            Are strong.
  Listen to the rhythm,
          The divine song.

Emanating from every pore,
   Every leaf, every drop,
    Coming from the roots,
      And making your soul sore.

-Su
@Beas

The Noise

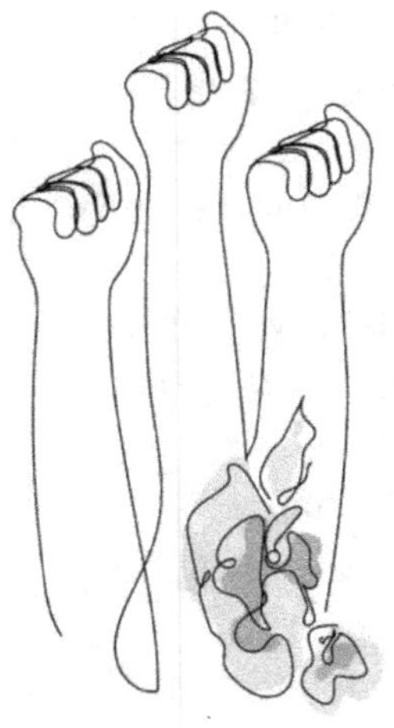

The noise
About feminism,
Liberation
From narcissistic patriarchy,

Holds true
For male liberation too,
From toxic patriarchy itself
And parasitic females.

Themselves—
To be able to express
From chains of conditioning,

Not to be slaves.

To be independent,
To take charge,
To not be a pest,

To be LOVE,

Instead of
Just an animal with lust,
And
A pronounced, scheming,
Greedy brain unjust.

Ultimately,
Not to be just a copybook—
Male or female,
Black or white,
Young or old,
Rich or poor,
Not a sheep in the herd
Of -isms,
But be intelligent,
Self-sufficient,
HUMANS.

Should be it.
-Su

Sorrow and love

Love and happiness
Sound like perfect companions.

Strangely, sorrow
Gave birth
Not to bitterness,
But to hope!

Sorrow and love—.
The odd couple—
Had courted each other,
Because there was 'faith'
That led one to the other,

To tie the knot
Knot, not in the relationship
But that, that strengthens the dainty rope
Chord umbilical to hope.

-Su

Moksha and dreams

Dreams are about hope,
A tingling, to look forward,
To imagine,
And create
A brainchild.
An aim
To walk and work towards.

Some are sweet,
Dreams,
Some are nightmares.

But
I worry,
When I attain moksha,
While the nightmares
Will evaporate—
Whoosh!

What will I do?
Sans my dreams!

Ohhh,
Moksha sounds boring.

-Su

Irritation

A constant irritation,
Left untreated,
Creates maladies chronic,
Cancerous!
Says the medic.

I tried,
Irritating
With rough sand
The smooth, silky membrane
Of a scallop, hardened by vagaries sick.

Back it gave
A pearl so rare,
Taught me the lesson—
The rare
may dare.

Receive the onslaughts
On the soul bare,
React, produce
No malignant scare.

But
For zillions to admire,
A timeless relic.

-Su

The Buddha moment

Sitting under a tree,
To the holy water's sound,
Faraway from the city's melee,
Or trudging onto a giant mound,

The Sage
Is not created
By all this or the passing years,
Or experiences the life grants.
They may be born
Or get emancipated—
It's nature's gift,
Not what a person wants.

The seed
Is in everyone.

At five,
They are geniuses all.
The passing years
May let it blossom,
Or chase after, to kill and maul.

The wisdom dawns,
Yes,
Everyone
Has the conscience.
Only those
Who value it
May Take their chance,
To open wide
The slit in the door,
Allow the faint ray
To fill, to pour.

The masses feel
Life would be dull, drab.
People might
See your honest innocence
Come after you to stab.

So, they keep the facade on,
Dare not remove the veneer
Of so-called smartness,
And lose all
In the simple life so dear,

And keep running after the mirage,
Like the proverbial deer.

-Su

Even Better

I never give
Perfect or ten on ten,
For, perfection doesn't exist.
You can always do better.

When the heart breaks
After a perfect love story,
Life is finished.
You never finish anything—
You can always do better.

When the best of health,
Mental alacrity,
Have passed by,
And life doesn't hold any joy,
With wisdom gained,
You can do…
even better!
-Su

From outdoors to in

The time when life comes to a standstill,
When everything and everyone beckons,
But one is stuck
In immobility.

Even the brain dreams
Of faraway places,
Of dear darlings.
It's time
To remove cobwebs,
Paint the indoors a spartan white,
Create an oasis, all-encompassing,
From networking to solitude.
Internalise, minimise,
Contemplate and you realise:

That nothing was needed,
All a facade, all surmise,
All, a race of mice.

Time! to prepare,
For that, that doesn't need
Even this minimum
To access the realm
Of the ultimate calm, stability, freedom—
Sans mind-body orchestration.

-Su

On my deathbed

I won't be sad
On my deathbed.

Life was not a bitch,
Bitter-sweet, but a nice mix.
It had a lot to teach,
From friends and foes,
Their own, to each.

Pain and pleasure,
Busyness, then vacuous leisure.
Relations came, relations went,
Some left scars, some a lingering scent.

Some shallow, some deep,
Some, for a lifetime to keep.
The life, but, was not for good—
All to leave, animosity, brotherhood.

Some took it to heart,
Loved not, they fought hard.
Win! Did they? What was to win?
All to leave, the noise, the din.

As it lasted, was a jolly ride.
By the rules, I too did abide,
All the while wondering inside,
What's the deal? Why the pride?

Then,
Came the inevitable,
The omnipresent,
The only Truth, stable,
The indelible presence.

Life came, life went,
Deathbed,
Never lost its eminence.

I'd slept through life, a restless sleep.
Now I'll take rest, uninterrupted, deep.
I could've done more, but regrets are none.
I came, I lived, I lost, I won some.

Everything in life is a win-win.
This dream, this drama, the impermanence,
A play, a farce akin.

-Su

Me

I've always searched
For a place
To call my own.

A name
That was mine,
That was 'me.'

Seeking from others
My glory,
My identity.

Then realised,
I am the place,
The soul inside

The statue.
That confined me,
Held me captive,
Trapped my wings,
Was not true.

I create.
I am the builder
Of the world.
I am the destroyer
Of the figurine
They had put
On a pedestal
To enshrine
In idolatry.

I am the continuum,
I am the pace.
I am
My own destiny.

-Su

Leaf to Leaf

Flitting from leaf to leaf,
Flailing limbs,
Falling from up above,
Face down, unhinged.

You took me for dead,
There's a lot of wind
Under my wings.

Vibrancy
Of soul,
To bestow
Zest and zing

To monochromatic
Mood swings.

.. Su

The night

I'm not a night's creature,
But
The night
I like more.

In its lap,
I rest finally,
In its immense possibility,
It is endless seemingly,
So homogenous,
So calm,
Its soothing tranquility.

It doesn't beckon

for action,
Yet the mind, the body,
Can usher more creation.

I weave dreams,
I can create that effervescent painting,
with its hidden songs
playing in the background.
I like the night's sounds.

Supine, I soar.
It's restful
and restive.
It's the night I adore.

-Su

SHAKTI

Grant them?
Equality, freedom, safety!
Who are they?
To grant?

When did women become beggars,
To seek grants petty?
The Goddess
creates the very existence of
the man that he boasts to be!

It is
Her love, her being
That's
HER own undoing.

But empathy, love,
Are respected
Only when an eagle spirit
Is behind the gentle dove.

Love is blind—
It's blinded her for too long.
Stop dancing to their tunes,
Be kind, but play your own song.

Show your claws, draw some blood,
Kali is also your name.
O Shakti, O Mother, compassion aflood,
You grant life; you can also maim.

Wake up—
Stop asking for doles.
Equality! You granted the unequals.
It's time to reframe some roles.

-Su

Longevity

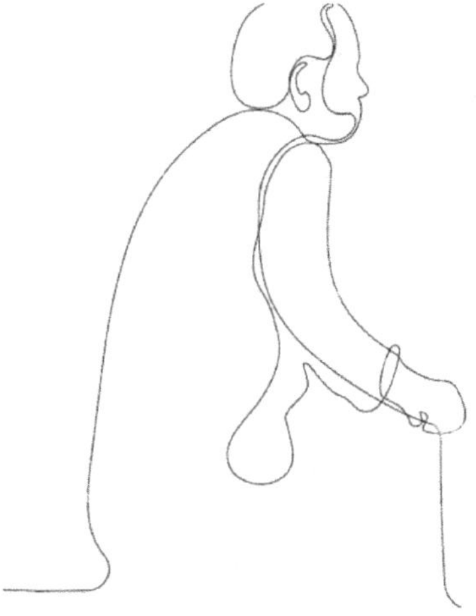

Is the lifespan really increasing?

Earlier, it was a hundred—
Natural, graceful, serene, kindred.

Now, they get parts changed
And pretend
To be active.
Superficial youth, superficial values—
Have found takers, are attractive.

Who has the patience
To be a *sanyaasi*

after fifty,
And teach the next generation
Under the tree?

They want fifty shades of grey,
No, not in the hair.

At seventy-five,
It's not the woods!
Beckons..
the power, the chair.
They don't evolve
beyond the livelihood,

The fallacy glitters, casts a spell,
A mirage? But it's hard to dispel.

-Su

Relativity

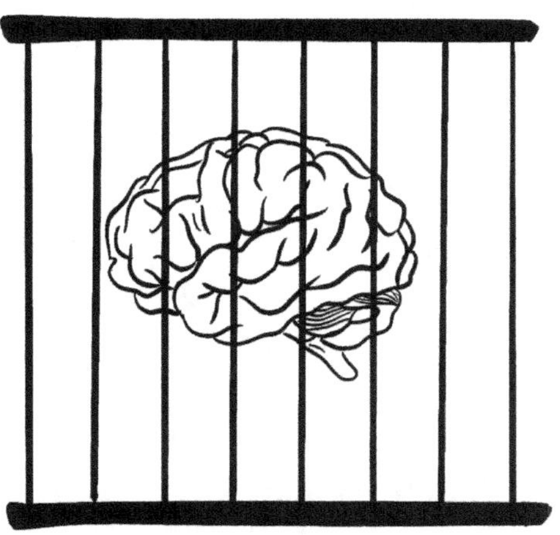

The theory of relativity!!
Oh how I love it!!!

One can lessen the pain by comparison,
One can heighten the glee by comparison.

There's so little time, so much to do,
Yet the 'moment' is so magnanimous—
One lives a lifetime through.

There's insatiable appetite for so much,
Yet the heart is full of contentment,
Ready to pull the plug and merge

Into the grand chasm
Anytime, any moment.

-Su

The Fable

You sink, you float,
The new takes over
From the old.

The mystic fable
Of the soul
Tells the stories untold.

The crests and troughs
Of life, so tough,
Transcended through

Yog—
Ever so soft, ever so bold.

It's the union
Of the Even,
Cosy warmth
Served always
With the odd cold.

-Su

Together, alone

Together?
But distant,
Miles, ages apart,
In their deeds, in their thoughts.

Is this marriage
Of convenience,
Greed, named Tradition,
Or hearts beating in unison,
Two souls creating a song
of ethereal transcendence?

Alone?
The two souls,

Dipped in love,
like crystal singing bowls,

Vibrating on their own,
Resonating, with the one,
Who is always there,
Yet considered,
Gone.

-Su

He blows hot he blows cold

HE blows hot,
HE blows cold,
His silvers
turn to gold.

The silky smoothness
After a rough storm,
The endless dark night,
And then, a sparkling dawn.

The blind curtain of despondency
Only to lift the spirits with
Scenic transparency.

Yes! I love His ever-changing consistency.

...And wait I do!
For His next colour,
His muted mattes
And exploding glossy vibrancy—
Some so shy,
Some so bold.

To take birth
From its ashes,
Ever evolving,
Never, to grow old.
-Su

Two Swans

Two swans,
Enamoured with each other,
Necks intertwined,
Dancing together.

But it was one.
The other was the shadow,
The love that one projected—
The ideal figure that she created,
Was her own.
She was love,
She was beauty,

She, the dancing queen,
She, the creator of life,
The nurturer of nature, the ideal wife.

In the placid water,
While there was calm,
All was dreamy,
All pure, in the dawn.

The harsh Sun of the noon,
removed the shadow.
In a moment,
She was her own widow.

Gently then,
Stretched the arm of the day.
The shadow elongated
For her to behold
To create another play.

She danced, twirled
Into the night,
Till the stars, the dreams,
Endowed her with might
To weave again
Some new rainbow streams.

-Su

Equation of love

Someone said—
In the equation of love,
If one leaves,
Nothing remains!

I asked,
Haven't you heard of
Unrequited,
Powerful
love,
Of Meera?

Who burned, glowed,
Illuminated Heavens
With
Love!!!

Why have we changed the definition?
Forgotten
The core, the meaning?

That
Love
Is…
Acceptance,
Surrender, glee,
In the other's being,
And ultimately
In one's own
Soul spring.

-Su

Nirvana here and now

Surprisingly,
There's no fear, of time running out,
No annoyance at fading colours,
No pain of loss,
No ecstatic meet-ups,
No madness of reaching, anywhere.
It's calm, quiet.
I view the world
From somewhere afar,
Watch with interest,
Grades of shades
Running a riot.

Moment to moment,
Living is fun,
Accepting love
From strange quarters,
Nothing to shun.
Wondering at their anguish and trying to
explain—
It's all fake.
But
No one seems to understand.
I tell myself,
Zip the lips
And chuckle within.
Why be glum?

-Su

End

A game—
You keep on playing.
The rules—
They keep on changing.
The ride—
You keep paddling.
The endeavour
To stay afloat—you keep scheming.

To what end?
Even the end

Doesn't justify the means.
By hook or crook,
You lived like a crook,
You survived.
To what end?
The same end?
In the end.

You say
You lived better.
Did you?
Live?
You pawned
Everyone, everything,
Felt like a puppeteer,
Pulling the string.
You thought you won the game,
In the end, you went
Just the same.

-Su

Life is a bicycle

They said,
Life's a bicycle. Keep paddling,
Or you shall fall.

I stopped,
Put the foot down,
And looked around.
I saw birds and flowers,
Trees and sunshine.
Thunder and showers,
Smiles all around,
In addition to mine.

The soothing moonbeams dancing
On rippling waters,
People of diverse origins,

Were not at each others' collars.

I found the lost kin,
Once pushed to the background
Of incessant rush, the mêlée,
The delicate relationships, life did pound.

Vanished like a haze,
Lure of lucre untrue,
The mirage of possessions,
That grew and grew.

Dawned a new dawn,
Of peace and tranquility.
I got off the bicycle
To find my own identity.

-Su

Suicide

I sink, I sail,
I live to tell the tale.
A wave of hope catches my arm,
In the midst of a blue storm.
I don't gatecrash a party,
Go uninvited, even to God's home.

I write thus and preserve
The cycle.
I ride the gust,
Paddle until the bike will take me,
Till it won't make me
Stop.

-Su

Rasa

It's green,
Serene, pristine,
Eyes shut.

I eye it,
With hope—
Of colour,

Vibrant, translucent, fragrant.

Today,
We both are silent.
Me—
Pregnant with expectant
excitement,
Of what could take birth,
The next moment.

It—
Placid,
Restful,
Content in its hibernation,
Oblivious
Of what could
Or could not be done.

There will be a dance—
Of life, of fragrance,
Of colour.
It shall unfold
Into magnificence untold,
By its sculptor.

It—
Is swaying
In *Rasa,*

The flow.
The mysteries—
Yet to grow,
Beyond any expectation,
Limited by knowledge-limited

In the depths,
Of potential, possibilities,
Unlimited.

-Su

A night swallowed

Another day,
A tiny ray,
A drop of Sun.
A night swallowed,
Evaporated.
The pride
Of the night,
Of Beauty imaginary,
The fluid intoxication in which it had wallowed.

The haystack,
The fluff,
Gathered over years,
The stuff
A cinder does it,

Bringing to ground
Without a sound,
The illusion
Of might—haloed.

Excitement gives way to realisation,
Bright, radiant.
Agape, you watch,
Through eyes narrowed.

The opposites attract.
Without night,
The day won't
Have the effect.
Lament not
The occurrences,
Ravel in grandeur bestowed.

-Su

The gift

The meteor
Burns out
In its rush.

But look
At the
Moon blush,
The Sun
Shining bright,

And in tones aflush.

Steadfast,
Permanent, immortal,
Disciplined,
In control, total.
Benevolent,
Not docile,
Turning the tides, seasons virile.

There's
Power in peace,
Inertia in speed,
Beauty in decay.
Be not a fool,
Abide by the rule
The creator lay.

Rush not, be kind,
Reach for the skies, but unwind.
Be one with Nature, God,
The games you play, need the nod.
The gift, they had you bequeathed,
Polish, chisel,
Vanquish greed.

-Su